MW00998100

We Go!

Planes

Dana Meachen Rau

Marshall Cavendish
Benchmark
New York

We go in a plane.

Planes go in the sky.

4

Planes go on water.

Planes go fast.

9

Planes have wings.

11

Planes have tails.

13

Planes have maps.

Planes have pilots.

We go in a plane!

Words to Know

map

pilots

sky

tail

water

wing

Index

Page numbers in **boldface** are illustrations.

About the Author

Dana Meachen Rau is the author of many other titles in the Bookworms series, as well as other nonfiction and early reader books. She lives in Burlington, Connecticut, with her husband and two children.

With thanks to the Reading Consultants:

Nanci Vargus, Ed.D., is an Assistant Professor of Elementary Education at the University of Indianapolis.

Beth Walker Gambro is an Adjunct Professor at the University of Saint Francis in Joliet, Illinois.

Marshall Cavendish Benchmark
99 White Plains Road
Tarrytown, New York 10591-9001
www.marshallcavendish.us

Text copyright © 2010 by Marshall Cavendish Corporation

Library of Congress Cataloging-in-Publication Data

Rau, Dana Meachen, 1971-
Planes / by Dana Meachen Rau.
p. cm. — (Bookworms. We go!)
Includes index.
Summary: "Describes the physical attributes, different kinds, and purposes of planes"—Provided by publisher.
ISBN 978-0-7614-4080-2
1. Airplanes—Juvenile literature. I. Title.
TL547.R352 2010
629.133'34—dc22
2008042510

Editor: Christina Gardeski
Publisher: Michelle Bisson
Designer: Virginia Pope
Art Director: Anahid Hamparian

Photo Research by Anne Burns Images

Cover Photo by *Corbis*/Michael Ochs Archives

The photographs in this book are used with permission and through the courtesy of:
Alamy Images: pp. 1, 9 Woodbridge Aviation Images; pp. 11, 21B Steve Gottlieb; pp. 13, 21TL Antony Nettle;
pp. 15, 20TL&TR gk photography. *Getty Images*: p. 3 Sam Bassett; pp. 17, 19, 20TL Digital Vision.
Corbis: pp. 5, 20B Maurizio Gambarini; pp. 7, 21TR Dale c. Spartas.

Printed in Malaysia
1   3   5   6   4   2